Looking at Our World

by Alison Adams

Table of Contents

What Does the World Look Like to You?

Do you think
it looks like this?

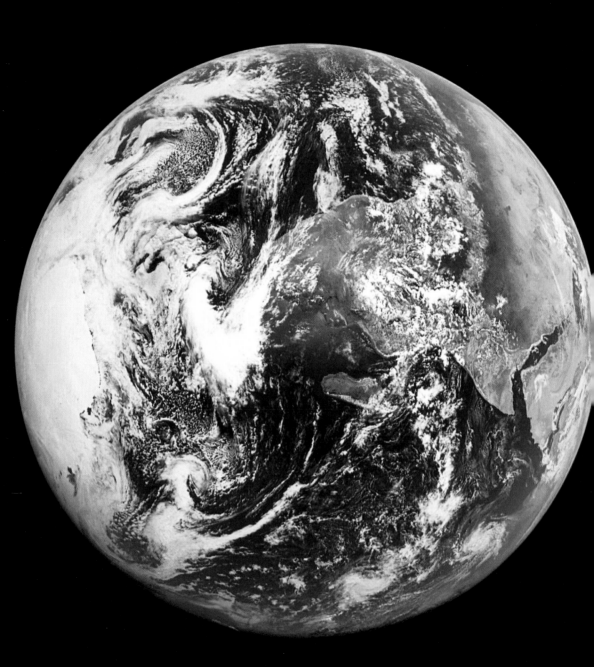

Do you think it looks like this?

Do you think it looks some other way?

People see the world in many ways.

What Did the World Look Like Long Ago?

A very long time ago, people thought the world was flat.
They thought they would fall off the end of the world if they went too far.

They thought there was only one big land with water all around it.

They thought that creatures were in the water.

They even thought a big turtle held up the world!

They thought these things long ago because they did not go very far from their homes.

Here are some of the people from long ago who helped us know more about the world.

The Vikings went by ship to areas in Europe and North America.

Christopher Columbus went by ship to the Caribbean.

Marco Polo went by land and by ship to China.

How Do We See the World Today?

Today we see the world in many ways.
We see the world
when we walk.

We see the world
when we go by car.

We see the world when we go by ship.

We see the world when we go by airplane.

Now we know what the world looks like from far away.

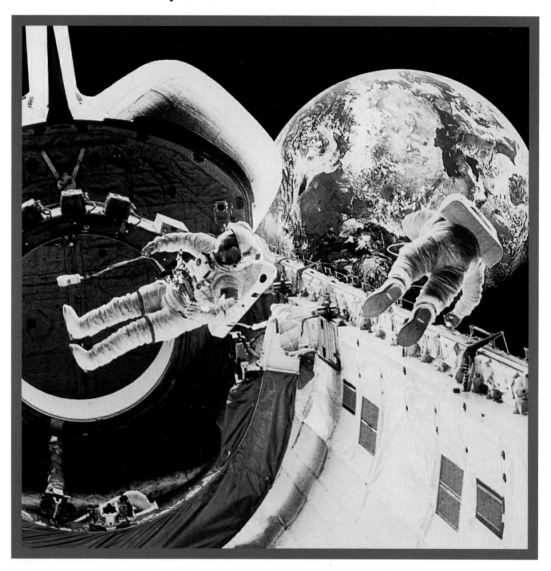